TO END A CONVERSATION

TO END A CONVERSATION

KELLY-ANNE RIESS

Edited by
Kent Bruyneel

thistledown press

Thistledown Press Ltd.
633 Main Street
Saskatoon, Saskatchewan, S7H 0J8
www.thistledownpress.com

Library and Archives Canada Cataloguing in Publication
Riess, Kelly
To end a conversation / Kelly-Anne Riess.
Poems.
ISBN 978-1-897235-54-6
I. Title.
PS8635.I48T64 2008   C811'.6   C2008-904525-4

Publisher Cataloging-in-Publiocation Data (U.S)
(Library of Congress Standards)
Riess, Kelly-Anne.
To end a conversation / Kelly-Anne Riess.
[64] p. : cm.
Summary: Poems that portray women in loneliness, longing and in the hands of often brutal lovers, but that also show the resilience of the human spirit to endure.
ISBN: 978-1-897235-54-6 (pbk.)
1. Women – Canada – Poetry. 2. Canadian poetry – Women – 21st century. I. Title.
811.6 dc22 PS3618.I4To 2008

Cover photograph (detail) by Taylor Leedahl
Cover and book design by Jackie Forrie
Printed and bound in Canada

10 9 8 7 6 5 4 3 2 1

 Canada Council
for the Arts
Conseil des Arts
du Canada
 SASKATCHEWAN
ARTS BOARD
 Canadian
Heritage
Patrimoine
canadien

Thistledown Press gratefully acknowledges the financial assistance of the Canada Council for the Arts, the Saskatchewan Arts Board, and the Government of Canada through the Book Publishing Industry Development Program for its publishing program.

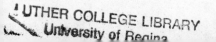

ACKNOWLEDGEMENTS

A special thanks to my mentor Steven Ross Smith for his editorial advice. Thanks also to the Sage Hill Writing Experience and the good people I met there. Instructors Karen Solie, Jeanette Lynes and Robert Currie's early encouragements were instrumental in the creation of this manuscript.

gillian harding-russell and James Trettwer also offered enlightened criticism on earlier drafts of these poems.

I am particularly indebted to the Erratics Writing Group (Alison Lohans, Bernadette Wagner, Marie Mendenhall, June Mitchell, Bonnie Flaman and Morgan Traquair) for helping me discover poetry's possibilities.

Thanks to those at the University of Regina who offered trenchant suggestions for my poetry, particularly Gerald Hill, Michael Trussler, and Kathleen Wall.

I am also grateful to my family and friends for their love and support.

My appreciation is also extended to the fine folks at Thistledown Press and my editor Kent Bruyneel for his insightfulness.

Earlier versions of some of these poems have appeared in the *Windsor Review, spring* and *Transition*.

The poem "The Scrape" alludes to "Mad World" by Tears for Fears.

For Andrew
How lucky we were to have something
that made it so hard to say goodbye

CONTENTS

EPILOGUE

Men get laid, but women get screwed.
— Quentin Crisp

Some people are settling down. Some people are settling. And some people refuse to settle for anything less than butterflies.

— Carrie Bradshaw, *Sex and the City*

Prologue

Hot Springs

follow me to the sea of round bellies
weave through thighs rippled by cellulite
dodge seniors sitting knee-deep along the edge
middle-age couples
don't cringe at the 400-pound Speedo-clad man
sit here beside me

touch me with fingers wrinkled
like clothes you forgot
to hang at the hotel
it's okay   we're among strangers
let's kiss until our skin
reddens and peels

Daffodils and Butterflies

Life after the Hill

When Jack and Jill were young, they dove from rooftops into strangers' swimming pools, back flipped from fences onto neighbours' trampolines.

A time of *I'll show you mine* and they did. Jill's grandpa gave them money for the convenience store. Jack and Jill sipped slurpees and chewed chocolate bars, sitting on the hill's backside in the park nearby. They looked at rock gardens and tidy lawns in neighbouring yards below, laughed uncontrollably at forgettable knock-knock jokes.

who's there
gopher
gopher who
gopher a walk with the dog, would ya
gopher it
gopher broke

It was a gopher hole that broke Jack's crown and Jill fell down right behind. She tripped over Jack, breaking her collarbone.

Now Jill's a doctor performing long hours for expectant moms. Jack stays home keeping kids and dishes clean. He likes Oprah and Dr. Phil, casserole left for Jill who returns late most every night while he's upstairs shampooing curly heads.

Jack has a bad back and Jill's knees are arthritic. They can't jump on a trampoline. They wouldn't risk the chance of falling now.

Loitering in a Booth at Dairy Queen

I eat salad   observe tattoos
spider webs on elbows of a boyish girl
flaming skull on her t-shirt
eating a chocolate-dipped cone
ten years older she'll be
embarrassed when her lawyer-lover
sees her arms   art in mutilation
ask me to show you scars
from when I was sixteen   cut up
from depression with
no cause   when the teen leaves

a boy and girl age five or six
move into her booth   wait for mom and dad
to bring cheeseburgers and fries
so cute with blonde hair
missing teeth   in ten years
they'll miss curfew   do drugs
or maybe they won't be cool
the boy picked on
stuffed in the recycling bin   rolled down stairs
maybe the girl will have BO   greasy hair
eat her lunches sitting on the toilet
locked away in a bathroom stall

next to the table two 30-something priests
religion still infects the young
I was born a cynic   I shook
my bottle at the roof and said
what kind of milk is this?

Fraction of a Hockey Date

she doesn't know much about hockey
except some boys in her class play

on skating trips she sits
in bleachers   multiplies
fractions   tries
to watch the game
but finds it boring
even more than fractions

she has a crush on Danny
who has black hair
wears Detroit
Red Wings t-shirts

Danny asks her on a date
junior worlds
all she understands is Canada
beats the U.S. 5 to 1
and hockey fans are annoying
with noisemakers
at least there is no fighting

on the walk home Danny rehashes the game
3:22 left on the clock
the U.S. trails

uh huh she interrupts

he stops
looks at her

then tries to kiss her

Blood Pressure and Eyeliner

grade 8s look so old
when you're grade 1
it's their permed hair   shaved legs
eyeliners   bras
high school is a distant place
lockers   cars   boyfriends   drinking   parties   drugs
so *Degrassi High*
when you're 14
20-year-olds are chic
apartments   university   office jobs with salaries
30-year-olds   40-year-olds   50-year-olds
oh so old and adult
cellulite   varicose veins   extra pounds
high blood pressure   low blood pressure
arthritis   cancer   heart attacks
70-year-olds   80-year-olds
cataracts   walkers   Alzheimer's   care homes
obits become the sports pages

when you're 25
30-year-olds   40-year-olds   start to look young
and teens so dumb when drunk
and 12-year-olds are too young
for boyfriends and kissing

Seen Again

i.

at my cabin I watch dragonflies finish
their hunt as the coyotes begin
their chorus out beyond the black
tree silhouettes   above a red moon
second night in a row

ii.

my dad used to say   I was Little
Red Riding Hood   I screamed
through the woods   dropped my basket
as the wolf sank its teeth
I was never seen again
except on *Unsolved Mysteries*

iii.

I told my boss I was sick today
some kind of flu   I can barely move
he believed me
probably imagined me in bed
with bucket at my side
instead I came out to the valley
for the chill tonight that's slipped
around my skin as I watch dragonflies
and remember what my dad said

iv.

when I was 16 in the park
with scrawny Daryl
his blue mohawk and blue eyes
in a water fight   Daryl doused me with a bucket
I picked up a water balloon
don't you dare
he said
back at school
I passed him in the hall and looked away
my dad didn't believe
Daryl shoved me to the ground

Emotional Damage Caused by Mixing Sex and Metaphor

it's not that she was saving it for marriage
rather just until she was done university
when she'd have a good job and be able
to support an accidental baby

then she met that raft guide
maybe it was his job or his muscular brown arms
there was no discussion

the snake stares out through open drawers
he slithers up her leg   fangs break through
blood trickles

she didn't object

he knew she'd take the bait
peels away
her skin   breaks off
ribs   rips out
her heart   tosses it
in the gut pile

she thought she'd try it
because everyone already had

she is one of many
broken and consumed

Sex and X

seX seX   seX
   X   X   X
   X an abbreviation for Christ

I wonder what X would say
back in his day about sex?

I think sex would be okay
with X

X
born of a virgin
born a virgin
hung
out
with a prostitute
(or was it his wife?)
some say
X had kids
what's a whore, dad?

is there anything wrong
with selling sex
X?

there's nothing new
why's sex taboo?
available at your corner store
or in an ad for jeans where
the model doesn't have to wear them
if you know what I mean

is there anything wrong
with selling sex
except for the disease?

the guy next to me in cubicle B
he's got HIV
why isn't he out
following some dream?
you could say the same to me —
though I'm healthy and clean

people die for sex   like
Romeo and Juliet
they died for sex   or was it
love?

make love   not war
people die from war
love and war
love and sex
sex and war
people die from sex
people die from war
people die for X
people die from crossing the street
probably being punished for having sex

From the Playground to the Gas Station

she told George
he was the ugliest of all the guys in fifth grade
George tried to speak
but felt his words
wiggle away

sometimes when George was with friends
she danced around them singing
loser patrol loser patrol
a cruel but tender war — all hurt and folly for George
fun for her
it wasn't that she hated him
actually if she was honest
she liked him   even though
George's tongue always fell flat
his words sluggish
she wasn't sure exactly what she liked

but he wasn't sluggish on the ice

years later she'd grown up   become flabby
her life dull   passing faster and faster
at the gas station
while getting a pop she saw George
by the cereal signing an autograph

she didn't dare say hello
her tongue had wiggled away

Tortola

if he slipped under the ocean
she wouldn't notice
too busy on the beach flipping through *Vogue*

she likes to tell her old classmates who suffer
the dry cold on Canadian prairies
how she digs her toes into sand
they're jealous but have no idea
of the floors she scrubs

he's not sure why she invited him
to the Virgin Islands
when she first came down
he couldn't come
because of her sun-kissed vision
of meeting a brown hunk

turned out it's not easy
for her to make new friends
they're intimidated
is what she said

so he dropped out
with the chance to go somewhere

under her mattress he found
a broken-framed picture
of himself which he contemplates
as he floats on his back letting waves push
his body to shore
where he later eats supper with her
watches the waxen lights of Tortola glimmer
digs his feet into sand
and wonders how long he'll stay

High School Reunion

I used to date him and hang out with his friends

we stole NO DUMPING signs
and placed them over toilets
we watched bad comedies and even worse
horror movies
we had dinner dates at Burger King
or Buffet Palace
our conversations — hockey this and baseball that

he seemed pretty good
but I had to lose him
and I did

he got into drugs after
high school
a year before
I started my Masters degree

I invited him for coffee once
he thought it was an intervention

there he is
look at him now
by the punch in that yellow suit jacket

I can't believe I ever dated him

watch
I bet he won't even come over to say hello

Cornered by Beowulf over Drinks

the JRR Tolkien translation
he's got a handlebar
moustache and it's 2006 for Christ's sake
he's teaching History 100
I think good for him
he said I should take his class
I said why would I do that
I'm taking English 840 in contemporary poetry
he said how nice like a pat pat pat on my head
then makes fun of initials behind my name
BJ as in Bachelor of Journalism degree
he said but the initials are BJ
I said that's because of the internship
he laughs   says someone told me you were funny
I half smile and wonder if euthanasia is
an acceptable way to end a conversation

A Photograph

we're all wearing aprons
even the men   one woman collects
aprons in our group   bought at Value
Village   she said
they're a fashion must
the large pockets in aprons are great
for holding pens and paper

we wrap our arms around each other
all of us standing in a row
I'm tucked under Karl's damp armpit
he's a poet who drives big trucks around oil rigs
on my right Malcolm's brown hand squeezes
my white shoulder tight
Malcolm paints basketballs with visual poems
about men who hunt on horseback with bows

there is Daisy the Catholic who likes to run
Kari whose husband from Israel can't sleep
after watching the news   Candice from
Zimbabwe ponders Munro's muse

our summer spent
writing about owls   cows
boyfriends   mothers   we're about
to say goodbye

in a few more years will I have forgotten
everyone's names?

That Someone

your cousin thinks you're a lesbian
your mother chastises   it's your
fault you're alone

there're no men no men no men
who aren't married or dumb
your dating life so dead —
sex feet under

then you find him
the FedEx man who visits your office everyday
his brown hair greasy glasses too big
his belly rounds out
his green sweater   he wears
the same white pants day after day

you don't have much
in common but he listens   remembers
details — like your cousin Mindy has a baby named Fred —
and it's good enough
you think

when he decides
to let you go   he stops
calling   you sit up late
cry into your e-mail —
I love you.
I need
someone.

A Clap of a Long Story

In my dream the tiles were green
or maybe grey
cold on my bare feet
I was locked in a small operating room
The doctors to harvest
my heart
give it to someone else
killing me
but you saved me
We escaped via bush plane

When I woke up
I had cramps   a sore throat
a headache

Perfume vial red with lust
vial red with passion
vial red with love
my beautiful poison

We had sex two times a day
 I don't care
about the other woman
There was another woman   right

I love you
Just let me
say it dear   Don't resist

You disappeared before my diagnosis —
the clap

My soul wants to go running
to you though you shamed me
I still want you
to love me

I put on a jacket   Go for a walk   Pretend
there is a hand to hold   Later make chili   Way too much
I sit across from a vacant chair

I watch the Friday night movie in the empty theatre known as
home
Lying on the green futon tattered wrapped in blankets —
substitute arms

Why do I miss you
You bastard —
My beautiful poison

Flushed

like wrapped saltine crackers in a dark cupboard
your boyfriend takes you out
to dump you in his soup

without removing the plastic he grinds
you down between thumb and middle finger
flakes and dust are all that's left

he tears the packet slowly and you
float down into a scalding mix
of soggy carrots and chicken bits

you ride the slosh down his esophagus
acid licks your skin   bounce off
stomach walls and slip along
the intestinal trail

Made for TV

those girls are ugly
          he said
not MADE FOR TV
          ugly
you know, the ones in REAL LIFE
who are cute, but on TV
          they're ugly

no, he said, those girls aren't MADE
                    FOR TV
                    ugly
     they're REAL LIFE
                    ugly
thanks, I said

Faces in Magazines

smell of Light Blue
perfume by Dolce and Gabbana
a sample between pages of women
in $990 Derek Lam asymmetrical seam skirts
and $348 Marc Jacobs quilted nylon jackets

make up and good light wipe out
blemishes and bags under eyes
airbrushing elongates necks
enlarges eyes   enhances cheekbones

everyday women
think men want to be with models (it's probably true)
repeat lots of reps
buy expensive makeup
starve
to try and be them —
these models in a mildewed magazine
tossed in a basement corner

That's Consumers good outline the way
People view you and they become part of
what you are.

Extra Pounds in Warm Blankets

an old-fashioned beauty
tugs and pulls
for some reason
the waistband of her skirt
can no longer slide
up her thighs

Renaissance nude
hops on the scale
twenty pounds
stuck to her butt
try the jeans
can't quite
squeeze   grab the sweats
and sigh

she worries no modern man will love her
vows zero carbs
two hours later has fries with friends
next morning she'll go
for a walk
but warm blankets smother
good intentions away
after work she plans to stop
at the gym
then remembers she forgot
to tape *Survivor*
far more important

Slim-fit and Shirtless in the Sun

he said he uses Oil
of Olay
three times a day

at work   he shows off his slim-fit
shirt bought in Venice
on a business trip —
he runs his hands down
his body

at home   he goes shirtless with a cowboy
hat on   the ring in his nipple
glistens in the sun as he
sits on the porch admiring
his TransAm — BADMOBILE
fully-loaded   leather seats
talking alarm —

watch
out   don't
get too close

The Men I Love

he looked like Angel
the guy from *Buffy*
seasons one two and three
totally hot   he came into the dojo
on Thursday nights   liked to tease me
tugging on my sleeve   Angel took me down
picked me up   fed me
encouragement when I didn't break
the board   he was married
during our karate demo in the park
I saw his wife Buffy
he would never leave for me
who'll always be a little fat

then there was that American lit
prof   read us Walt Whitman
I knew what I wanted to do
after a few *Leaves of Grass*
he could be my wound
dresser   I don't care if it hurts his knees
ratemyprofessor.com
no I'll date my professor
except I know better

and then there was you love
my first love
taught me everything I know about sex
told me you loved me while rubbing sunscreen
on my back then packed me on the bus
I found a card at the bottom
of my bag   *goodbye don't call*
it'd make you feel bad

Secret Desire of a Fly

she buzzes around parties for conversational scraps
helps herself to the snacks   wishing
she didn't have to spit to break up food
no wonder they swat at her

it would be better if she could transform
with two legs   two arms and a mouth full of teeth
she could chew a whole piece of cake
sip on a glass of wine without falling in
be surrounded by people who want to talk to her

Young Hires

Kathy sleeps in until seven
then fumbles around
making her ten minutes late
no one minds
as long as she brings coffee

Kathy moved from Moose Jaw to Montreal
to take a marketing job
she's on the safety committee   social committee
was conned into union rep
everyone in the building knows her
she's been at it a year
hasn't met anyone her own age

Kathy's closest friend Bob is 48
gets around
in a wheelchair
doesn't let anything stop him
except stairs and narrow parking stalls

well, well, well
Bob greets her
before they go for lunch every day
to talk about the latest episode of *Six Feet Under*
the deadly crash on the six o'clock news

what an idiot   Bob says
about the man who runs over his own head
how does anyone do that?
about the woman who ramped her car
into McDonalds

through the grapevine Kathy hears Bob
fell trying to reach an open window
his keys on the bedside table

made him a born-again cynic
I don't know   I don't care
and it doesn't make any difference
he quotes Kerouac all the time

Bob's dream is to wheel himself
on the track of the Tour de France
causing cyclists to crash
did they just hit a man in a wheelchair
the announcer would ask

sometimes Kathy thinks she's in love with Bob
which is why every time the company fires
Kathy wishes for a young male hire

The Weight of a Man

you will not suffocate
if the elevator stalls you read
while going down
think of your best friend
who told her boyfriend (who never dresses
up for a date) she wanted
a break   he took up
time she needed for her thesis
and he didn't assemble
her new bed frame
drank with friends instead

splish splash on a Saturday night
three poetry books stacked by the tub
for you to thumb
rub a dub dub

later you lie face down
on your bed   wrapped in a towel
your cat licks water off the back
of your knee and you sigh
missing the weight of a man

you will not suffocate

Downtown I Circle around Eight Blocks
Searching for a Parking Spot

I am
high heels and lipstick with thrift store style
twenty-eight falling asleep in an office
painted white peeling like dead
skin chapped by dry air
paper stacks on a dusty desk
I dream of an affluent life away from pasty
bosses with sausage-fat limbs who crumb
creativity like dried bread

before I leave   I check my e-mail
nothing from friends
only Xanax spam

the wind's icy fingernails stab
into my thighs as I walk
to my car

back home I don't get off the couch
until it's too late to eat breakfast
again

On the Swing

By the chips, a man
in red Santa cap, stares at the woman dressed
as a French Maid.   Pumpkins illuminate
the crowded room.   She paid
$20 at Wal-Mart for the short black dress

She'd noticed him before
renovating her office,
had seen him watching her.

Now he's at the party alone.   Encouraged
by liquor, she approaches, says hello
then turns to leave. He follows her,
places his hand on her waist, says nothing more.
Snow fills streets on the walk to her place.
Inside, on the coarse rug,
he slips off
her shoes.

The next morning she finds a note
on her pillow: *Thanks for the good time*.

On Sunday, she saunters
home from church.
She stops.
He's in the park
pushing a toddler on the swing.
At his side, a pencil-thin woman pokes out
from underneath a super-sized pea coat.

Back at the office, on Monday, he dashes by
digging through his toolbox while she types.
Her posture perfect.

Apples and Eve

red delicious   granny   crab
why the apple so tempting
not as sweet as a berry —
rasp   straw   blue

I'm blue
with this idea
paradise lost —
running around nude
through the garden
is that all
to paradise?

The Apple?

me bruised but I did not fall
to the ground
rather into a soft bed
another one night stand

no one needs marriage
to justify love
to justify sex

the apple
that bonded woman to man

one bite
and women couldn't work or vote
one bite
brought women monthly bleeding and cramps
pain in child birth
Eve's punishment
or so the legend goes

I'll obey no man even so
I watch and wait for blood
to tell me there will be no miracle
no new life

my apartment silent
no pattering of feet
only the rattle of the radiator
the humming of the fridge
in its bottom drawer a whole bag
of red delicious

Half-soaked in Beer

it's that stuffed bear I took from the bar
reminds me of you
I'm not sure how it got there
half-soaked in beer like us
because you spilled your Labatt twice
switched to red wine
and splashed on your white shirt

we walked the hills   tripping over gopher holes
found a fire hydrant in a field
you said you liked my checkered underwear
blades of grass left red marks on your cheek
dew beaded your face
the speed of your chest
rising up and down
slowed then stopped

the stuffed bear
now face down on my coffee table
reminds me of you

Luck in the Battersea

My favourite restaurant. The Battersea Tandoori.
Its chai and naan are divine.
I go there a few times a year.
The last time for a celebration of me.
Dipped a long pink sleeve into butter chicken
reaching for thirds.

Our server's name was Lucky.
My water glass never empty.
His family owned the Battersea.
Lucky wore a silver bracelet.
His religion Sikh.
Lucky liked to party.
He said hydration was key.

Lucky's girlfriend served at the Battersea too.
It was serious.
They texted 25 times a day.

I left the Battersea
to launch my latest novel at the reception.
Lucky went out with friends.

I received two bouquets of flowers that night,
and a meager reading fee.
Lucky got hammered.

Saskatchewan in Love

he could never love
her — flat barren cold
it's not windy until the roof lifts off
she'd say like it's a joke

he was a mountain
beautiful from a distance
because he was there   she wanted to climb
he let her summit   admire the view
before shrugging her off
she screamed all the way down
fractured when she hit the ground

he couldn't love that girl in the armpit
of Canada   the easiest province
to draw   he wasn't into distance
she shrank
in the rearview of his pickup

If I Gave Up

I would have followed you
to Edmonton
found a job waitressing   babysitting
even though I have three degrees

a temporary fix
while you finished school
near mountains where you climb

I wish I'd known you
when you didn't know what you wanted
then maybe you would've followed me to the Peg
I *could never live in Manitoba*   you said
would feel bad if I gave up
anything for you
so you ended it

even so   you couldn't stay away
visited me every summer
until she moved in

after graduation you went up north
how's that better than Winnipeg
you work 20 days on
fly down to her on days off
it could be me

A Kiss From the Door

your breath pulses against the back of
my neck   dead weight
of your arm draped over me
like the tentacle of a dead sea beast

your alarm screeches awake   your lips push
against mine   before you jump up
throw pants over legs
shirt over head
blow me a kiss from the door

your day will be spent packing
tourists plump like bullfrogs aboard buses
stuffing them in wetsuits   I'll be packing
to head home by Greyhound   before she gets back
from Spain   this was the last time
you said   *it's time*
to move on

my phone will ring a week
from now   hearing your voice
I'll breath in

Awaiting an E-mail from Summer

winter lingers
like loneliness my frigid fingers ignite
friction defrosting my thighs
dulls the ache
yearning for summer
like a lover in Madrid
and me in Hella   awaiting an e-mail
a phone call
some sign he exists
that he'll come back
remove my toque
peel away my long johns
press his warm freckled skin on mine

Daffodils and Butterflies

you compared my poems to Raymond Carver's
mocked the way I plucked cucumbers and tomato
onto my plate *I'm sick of lettuce*
I complained   later I found
a lettuce head in my bed
I returned it to your toilet
tragic abuse you said *kids are starving*

we ignored each other after that
locked in sessions
then me working in my room at night
you out drinking in the bar

until our day off   you invited me to the hotel
pool   floated on our backs
I told you the story about swimmers
who died in the world trade centre
you spent the whole afternoon Googling
to find out it's a lie   your revenge
fill my shower with balloons
I popped them   dumped them
in your toilet *tragic abuse* you said
kids are starving   I love you
I wanted to say but the words clung to
my throat   thank God

we ignored each other after that
locked in sessions
then me working in my room at night
you out drinking in the bar

now it's the day we leave
I offer you a ride to the airport

what are we going to say on the way
what kind of goodbye do you want
can I dump you outside the terminal
say I'll e-mail sometime
do I shake your hand
do I park the car
plug the meter

okay

who knew it'd end like this
with you in my arms   I ask
should this be a scene with daffodils and butterflies?
I'm not sure what I mean

butterflies are bastards is your reply
no one knows what they do in those cocoons

Places I Awoke

I dreamt you took
my poem broke
my lines in ways they shouldn't
be broken
Added turquoise
in random
places I woke
screaming: *I am*
a contemporary
image poem!

I dreamt we were back at that conference where we first met. I
tried to tell you I loved you but a fat witch tied me down, broke
my face with her fist.

And last night I dreamt your wife died. You collapsed at my side
and cried. I reached down, ran my fingers through your hair. You
swatted me away, knocked me downstairs.

I woke not knowing where I was, but your arms around me told
me we were still at the hotel. I drifted back to sleep wondering if
your wife dreamt about daffodils and butterflies.

Eve's Rib

I won a trillion dollars
for best poem
there were 10 such awards given away
by the University of BS

I dreamt after we left
the conference where we met
we stayed in touch by telephone
you visited every chance you had
one day dumped *love you* on my head

when we decided to get together
it wasn't cheating because your red-headed wife had already left
you and I planned a trip to New York

when I wake up the balance in my bank account
remains the same
$85
you and I are so similar   I have no doubt
you're my estranged rib married in PEI

Pegged

you asked me to drop
$400   fly east
before Christmas holidays

it's not working between you and what's her name

I meet you at the stratigraphy conference
while you're locked away listening
to talk about strata and topographical maps
I'm alone in this hotel room

golden boy stares down
through my window
sees me   wearing a t-shirt
bare-legged in underwear
holding a hot chocolate
I'm waiting for you to be done
she's waiting for you to come back home

the city's ornaments —
angels and stars — glow
with colours of Christmas
green — the colour of money
red — the colour of flames

you ask me if tomorrow
while I'm waiting
if I would mind picking up
a gift for what's her name

what's the colour of anger?

Tucked Under

Josh looks
12 but is 31
a rocker guy once a comic book kid
tucked under sheets reading
with a flashlight

he wears glasses that wouldn't win
a schoolyard fight
but he gets off on Lily's teasing
jabs   he tells her she's beautiful
when she's mean

Lily looks angry but is sad
for Josh will not leave
the wife he loathes —
Chloe who he met at 15
a red head he could pick out of the crowd
without his glasses   Chloe's the mother of his son
another comic book kid
Chloe and Josh conceived when they were 18

the woman Josh really loves he met at 31
will keep him only in memory
tucked under her sheets

Back into Her Life

for two years she let him play her
like spoons against his knee
until a postcard of New Brunswick
depicting the Carleton Martello Tower
the postmark said Jamaica
his scrawl *Goodbye*

but it wasn't long
until he barged
back through her door
with an engagement ring

he found her sitting naked on the sofa
brushing her hair   when she pushed
him out   he waited
she always had trouble saying no to him

the ring fit a little too tight
thirty-four and engaged with a price —
he asked her
to leave the prairies
her job as a teacher
her mom and dad
follow him to the mountains
where all she'll have is him
working at his gallery

while he waits for her answer
he insists she pose for one of his art projects
he wants to photograph her wearing nothing but a life
jacket   she insists on a long shirt underneath
after the first flash of the camera   she contemplates the *clink*
the ring would make if tossed to the floor

Have You Heard This?

words tail each other like ants
foraging for a home   these words
looking for the page
looking for the book

I'm stuck he says
when he tells me he couldn't make
my poetry slam   I hear
from a friend his wife (who I didn't know
existed until now)
doesn't like it when he goes out

and sometimes
have you heard this?
words run away   hide between legs
when needed most

but these words like ants on a poem
are frustrations I feel
an e-mail to be sent   an ant
on a dish to be washed
I want you to know me

have you heard this?
I want to be close to you
to show you I'm cool   know a lot
well not a heck of a lot
other than who won *Survivor*   every season

Remembrance Day 2006

she looks forward to the stat holiday
a chance to catch up on cleaning
her carpet hasn't been vacuumed
dust
grows thick on her bookshelf   morning

comes   she opens the door to
forty-two
faces of men on the front
page of the newspaper
dead   in Afghanistan

she scrubs her own kitchen floor
on hands and knees   remembers
last fall   visiting her cousin
and the unknown soldier
he died in France   the First World War
buried at Vimy   later
shipped to Ottawa
sealed in a granite tomb
which she stood atop
took a picture
while others knelt and prayed

Hi Suzanne Hi

he's hard-boiled eggs on
toast with a slice of cheese
and a glass of milk
what she really wants is the other guy   musk
melon served with Cinzano Rosso

she meets musk melon
guy at her office
word is he's a ballroom dancing teacher
by night   she tries not to stare
at meetings but he sits across from her
hi Suzanne hi
he says forcing her to look

she and her eggs on toast watch
Jeopardy each night shouting
out answers and yes keep score

she used to go out with her girl-
friends until she met egg man
bars are too noisy   he said
she feels guilty
leaving him alone
so she stays with him
watches the world go by
can't free herself
and no one will free her

she imagines musk melon doing
the east coast swing to "Mustang Sally"
a-one   a-two   one   two
the only weepin' eyes would be egg man
if he were capable of stepping out

Last Breakfast at Home

Inside, Edith does crosswords with her one good eye, sits close
to the TV to hear the six p.m. news. She goes to bed at seven,
gets up again at five, sets her hair, gets a muffin crumb in her one
good eye; it brings tears. Later, she drops cantaloupe seeds on her
foot.

Edith's life is packed, boxes in her living room. Tarot cards
are scattered across the coffee table mixed with newspapers.
Underwear and wet towels wait to be picked up off the bathroom
floor. Her dishes need to be done. She's still in the sweats she
wore yesterday. The movers will be here at noon.

A Poem for the New Millennium

they said the world would end in 2000, whoever *they* are

I got a Y2K bug
a green hornet
as a Christmas gift
it sounded like shattered glass
when you dropped it

I thought there would be
terrorist attacks when the ball dropped
in New York
in Times Square

I stayed home that New Year's
all I remember was an empty bottle
of wine heavy in my hand

seven years later   4 months 27 days
the batteries will be dead
in that Y2K bug

I saw the man my sister will marry
I know the next car my parents will buy
I saw the person I will become

there's no turning around

Epilogue

The Scrape

The dreams in which Jennifer is dying are the best she's ever had.

Jennifer doesn't like getting on airplanes and therefore hasn't seen the world.

When Jennifer drives her children to soccer then Girl Guides, she sees her car crashing into the school bus. Metal on metal, hears the sound of the scrape.

All Jennifer had accomplished were her children and avoiding the sweet scraping sounds of colliding with the bus.

Jennifer imagines her parents getting old and what it might mean for her.

DATE DUE

OCT 0 6 2009	